Ralph Masiello's

CHRISTMAS

DRAWING BOOK

Charlesbridge

For Lauryn and John, who love Christmas—R. M.

Also in this series:

Ralph Masiello's Ancient Egypt Drawing Book

Ralph Masiello's Bug Drawing Book

Ralph Masiello's Dinosaur Drawing Book

Ralph Masiello's Dragon Drawing Book

Ralph Masiello's Fairy Drawing Book

Ralph Masiello's Farm Drawing Book

Ralph Masiello's Halloween Drawing Book

Ralph Masiello's Ocean Drawing Book

Ralph Masiello's Robot Drawing Book

Other books illustrated by Ralph Masiello:

The Dinosaur Alphabet Book

The Extinct Alphabet Book

The Flag We Love

The Frog Alphabet Book

The Icky Bug Alphabet Book

The Icky Bug Counting Book

The Mystic Phyles: Beasts

The Skull Alphabet Book

The Yucky Reptile Alphabet Book

Cuenta los insectos

Published by Charlesbridge
85 Main Street
Watertown, MA 02472
(617) 926-0329
www.charlesbridge.com

Library of Congress Cataloging-in-Publication Data
Masiello, Ralph.
    Ralph Masiello's Christmas drawing book / Ralph Masiello.
        pages cm
    ISBN 978-1-57091-543-7 (reinforced for library use)
    ISBN 978-1-57091-544-4 (softcover)
    ISBN 978-1-60734-656-2 (ebook)
1. Christmas in art—Juvenile literature. 2. Drawing—Technique—Juvenile literature.
I: Title. II. Title: Christmas drawing book.
NC968.5.C45M37 2013
741.2—dc23   2012037573

Printed in China
(hc) 10 9 8 7 6 5 4 3 2 1
(sc) 10 9 8 7 6 5 4 3 2 1

Illustrations done in mixed media
Display type set in Couchlover, designed by Chank, Minneapolis, Minnesota;
    text type set in Goudy
Color separations by KHL Chroma Graphics, Singapore
Printed and bound July 2013 by Jade Productions in Heyuan, Guangdong, China
Production supervision by Brian G. Walker
Designed by Susan Mallory Sherman and Whitney Leader-Picone

Season's Greetings, Jolly Artists!

Is there anything more magical than Christmastime? When I was a kid, I daydreamed about Santa, Mrs. Claus, tinkering elves, and airborne reindeer. I also wondered if I would be on the Naughty or the Nice List. (Somehow I made the Nice List each year.)

In this book, I want to give you a Christmas present—the gift of art. I will show you how to draw Santa's sleigh, elf-made toys, and a decorated tree. As you learn to illustrate snowmen and stockings hung with care, I hope that you'll be warm and cozy.

Follow the steps in red to create your drawings. Then color in your artwork with your favorite tools. Try the extra challenge steps in blue to make your art even more merry and bright.

May your Christmas be filled with joy, peace, and drawing!

Ralph

Choose your tools

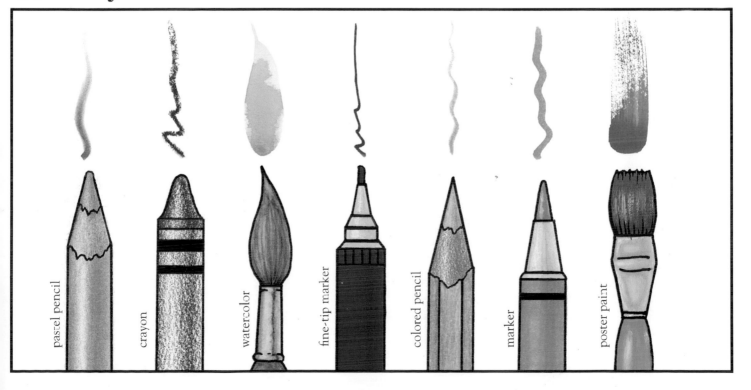

pastel pencil crayon watercolor fine-tip marker colored pencil marker poster paint

Snowman

Snow Woman

Decoration Station

Christmas Tree

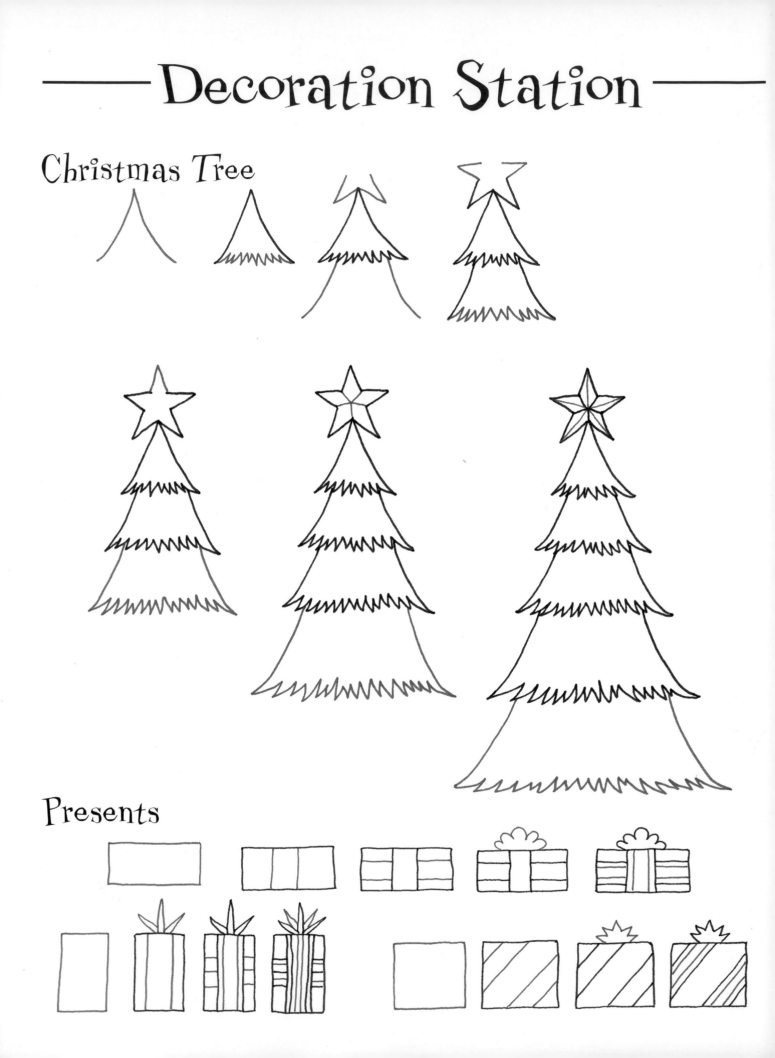

Presents

String of Lights

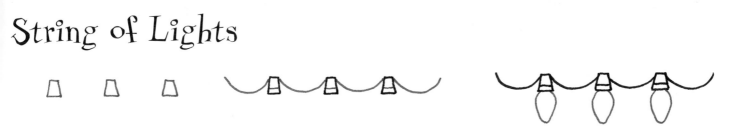

Ornaments

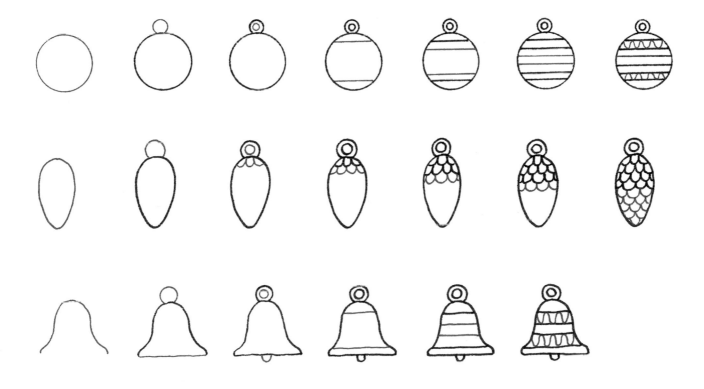

Wreath

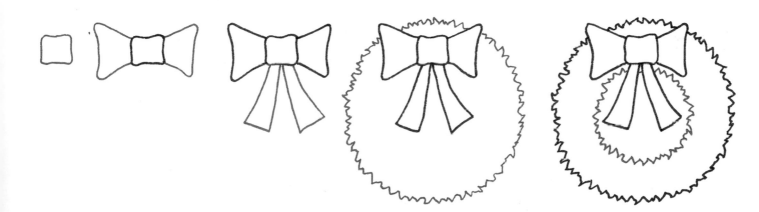

Fireplace

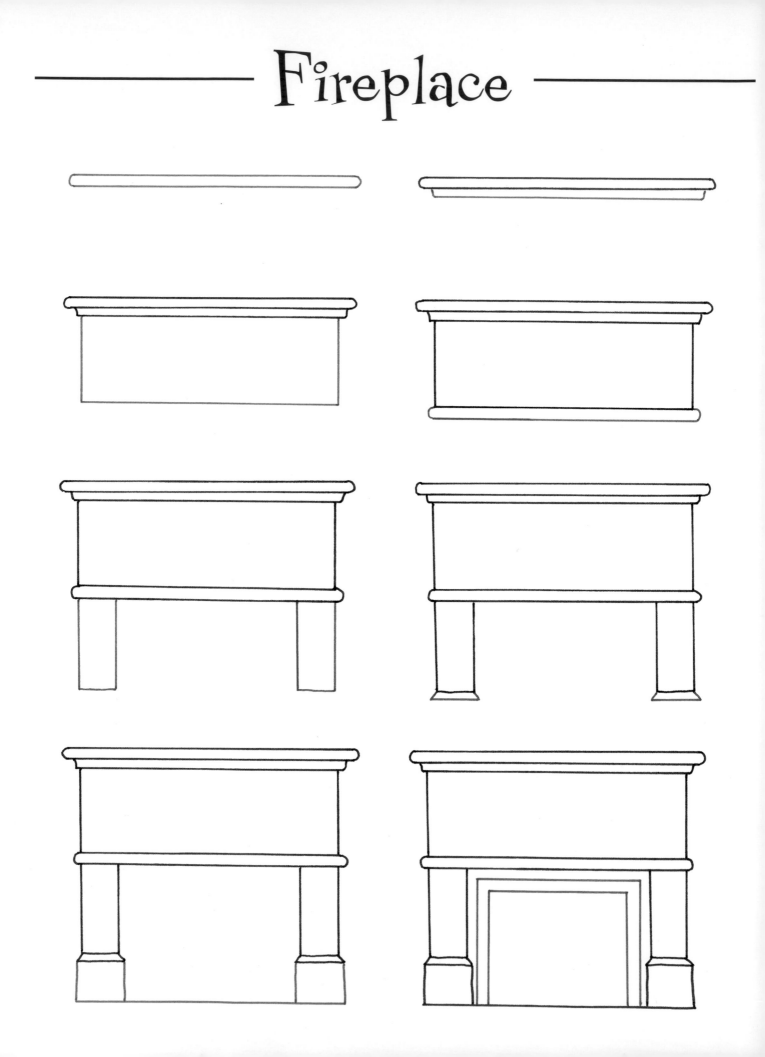

watercolor, marker, and colored pencil

The stockings were drawn
by the chimney with care.

Santa Claus

North Pole

NICE

NORTH POLE

Mrs. Claus

Holly

Take a stroll at the North Pole.

watercolor, marker, and colored pencil

Elves

Screwdriver

Paint Brush

Hammer

Toy Workshop

Workbench

Train

Robot

Teddy Bear

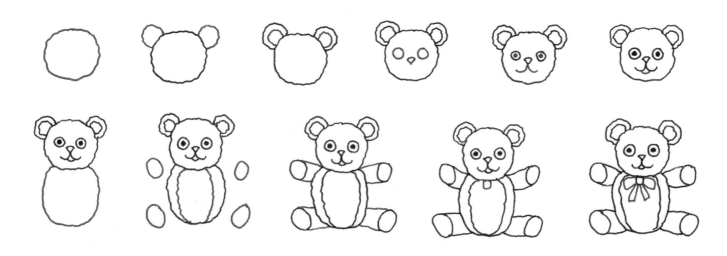

These elves are gifted!

watercolor, marker, colored pencil, and crayon

Santa's Sleigh

Reindeer

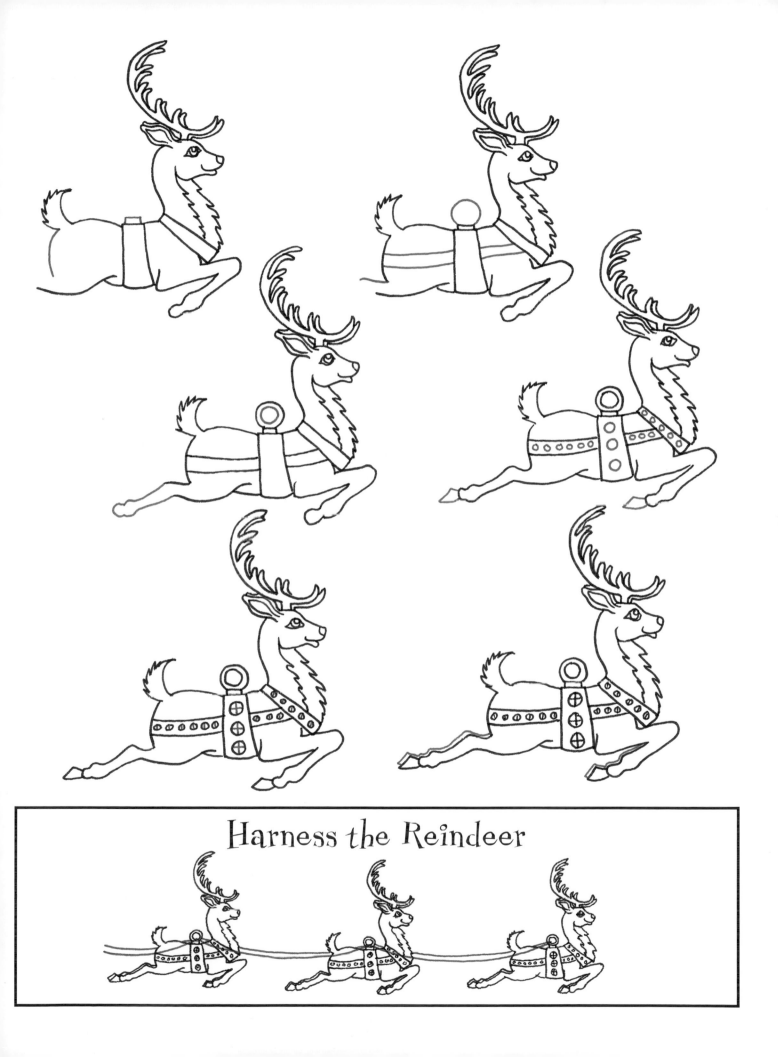

Harness the Reindeer

House

Town Houses

Brownstone

Roof Styles

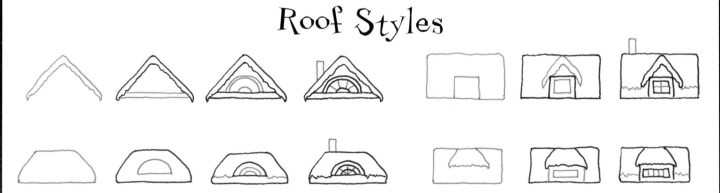

Clock Tower

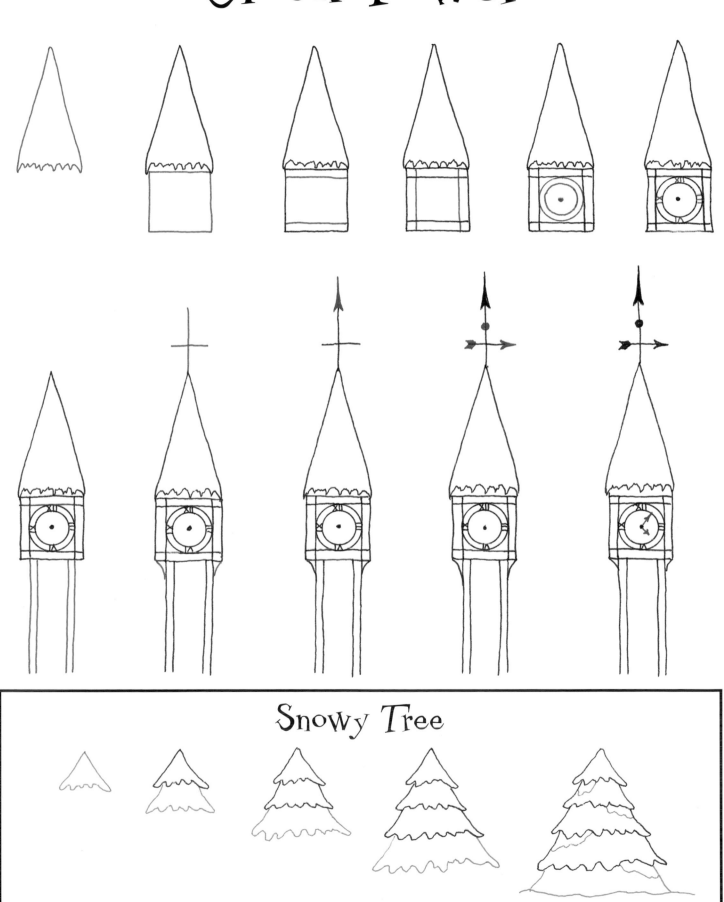

Snowy Tree

Merry Christmas to all, and to all a good night!

watercolor, marker, pastel pencil, and poster paint

Resources

Books

Barry, Robert. *Mr. Willowby's Christmas Tree*. New York: Doubleday Books for Young Readers, 2000.
A Christmas tree proves too large for Mr. Willowby.

Biedrzycki, David. *Santa's New Jet*. Watertown, MA: Charlesbridge, 2011.
Santa may need to fly a fancy jet when his reindeer are too out of shape.

Moore, Clement C. *The Night Before Christmas*. Watertown, MA: Imagine/Peter Yarrow Books, 2010.
The classic poem celebrates the anticipation of Christmas.

Suess, Dr. *How the Grinch Stole Christmas*. New York: Random House Books for Young Readers, 1957.
The Grinch tries to steal Christmas from Who-ville but is surprised by the holiday's true meaning.

Sullivan, Robert. *Flight of the Reindeer: The True Story of Santa Claus and His Christmas Mission.*
   New York: Macmillan, 1996.
Photographs, illustrations, and statements from zoologists, scientists, and explorers set out to prove that Santa is no myth.

Tillman, Nancy. *The Spirit of Christmas*. New York: Feiwel & Friends, 2009.
In jolly verse, the magical traditions of Christmas are celebrated.

Waddell, Martin. *Room for a Little One: A Christmas Tale*. New York: Margaret K. McElderry Books, 2006.
Join Kind Ox and his animal friends as they welcome Mary and Joseph into a warm stable.

Websites

Christmas Games
www.primarygames.com/holidays/christmas/games.php
Load Santa's sleigh, find Frosty, or spot the stocking surprise in a virtual world of holiday games.

Easy Christmas Crafts
www.littlefamilyfun.com/2012/11/christmas-crafts.html
From egg-carton snowmen to Santa puppets, enjoy simple, fun crafts for all ages.

Handmade Ornaments
www.parents.com/holiday/christmas/crafts/handmade-gifts/
Lots of ornament ideas for trimming the tree.

Homemade Holiday Gifts
www.parentmap.com/article/15-homemade-christmas-gifts-that-kids-can-make
Craft some handmade gifts such as bookmarks, plant holders, felt necklaces, and more.

Kid-Friendly Christmas Cookies
www.bhg.com/christmas/cookies/christmas-cookies-for-kids
Bake chewy chocolate reindeer or sugar-cookie carolers.